BARSTOOL ORIGAMI

THE ART OF TURNING SOBER PAPER INTO BOOZY CONVERSATION PIECES

NICK ROBINSON

UNIVERSE

Contents

Introduction

WHAT IS BAR STOOL ORIGAMI?

Ask five ordinary people what they consider to be the best bar game. The chances are, the answers you'll get will be anything from darts to dominoes, foosball to cards. However, these people are all wrong... The best bar game by several light years is origami.

As an art-form, origami goes back, oh, ages. Often it's used to create recognizable objects, sometimes abstract conceptual pieces (such as "origami boulders") and sometimes, entertaining games. With the exception of a few basic folds, there are no rules to learn, and it's incredible just how much fun and mischief you can get from the simple combination of a sheet or two of innocent paper and your own two hands. Plus, people will think you are clever and talented. You'll charm the opposite sex and members of the same sex will bask in your reflected glory... Probably.

You'll find out with experimentation which designs work best with which kind of paper, although in an emergency, you can make

them all from almost any type of paper. They will look much more impressive if you use some bright or patterned paper, so get on down to your local art or craft store and invest heavily. Serious folders will naturally wish to buy some "proper" origami paper.

There are a few proverbs that you ought to know before tackling the designs in this book, so please memorize the following gems:

- Like beer, if you fold too much, too fast, you'll regret it.
- Damp paper is not happy paper.
- Little mistakes at the start become big ones later on.
- It's a wise man who pre-creases his sinks.
- Paper is as paper does, then it tears.
- If at first you don't succeed, have another drink.
- A bird with a broken wing can sing, but you can't pluck feathers from a frog.

The last one requires an intermediate schooling in Zen philosophy to properly appreciate, but it's helped me through some tough times. On a more practical point, the best thing to remember is to fold slowly and

neatly. You should also make each design several times at home before considering whether to unleash it upon a waiting world (or bar). By the time you've made it five times, it'll start to look good enough to impress all of your friends.

Before trying out your favorite designs in a live environment (i.e. down at your local bar) you may wish to consider taking out personal insurance. Neither the author nor the publishers can be held responsible if you need dental work after getting on the wrong side of your local, aggressive drunk, or her boyfriend, who doesn't appreciate origami.

If you're interested in pursuing origami as a hobby (I don't recommend it as a full-time career), there are huge amounts of information to be had on the internet and origami societies exist in almost all civilized countries.

TECHNIQUES YOU'LL NEED

Paper-folding diagrams for any type of origami use a standard set of symbols that allow people to follow instructions, even in another language. Here are the basic symbols you will need for this book:

Valley fold – the paper is folded upwards and you can make this fold with the paper flat on the table. The arrow shows where to fold from and to.

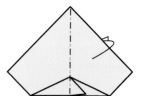

Mountain fold – the paper is folded underneath. You do this "in the air" (i.e. off the table) or turn the paper over and carry out the fold as if it were a valley crease.

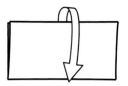

Pull the paper out – there are often hidden flaps, which may need gently pulling out, or it may be used to mean unfold the last few steps.

Reverse fold – Some folds are "reversed" so that the paper folds back inside itself. Study the diagrams carefully!

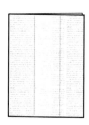

Fold and unfold – double-headed arrows indicate where to fold to and then unfold.

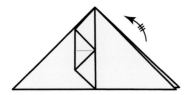

Repeat – a fold arrow with a small dash across it means you need to repeat a move, usually symetrically on the other side of the paper.

Existing crease – where a crease is made and unfolded, it leaves (gasp) a crease line.

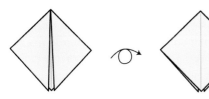

Turn the paper over – flip the paper like a pancake!

TIPS FOR FOLDING

- Always fold with clean hands on a flat surface, such as a table or a large bar stool.
- Try to lick most of the beer off the surface before folding.
- Fold in a quiet bar, free from disturbances.
- Don't try to drink whilst folding (although before and after is fine!).
- Check the next step so you can see how it's supposed to look, even if you've absolutely no idea of how to get there.
- Try as you might, potato chip bags do not fold well.
- A beautifully folded item of origami can sometimes be exchanged for free drinks. It's worth doing it for this alone!
- Read the words, they can help a lot.
- If the design is complex, don't try to fold it at the end of the night.
- Don't expect origami to help you meet that "someone special"—it just won't work.
- Make each design three times before moving on, each will be much better than the last and it will also help you memorize the sequence.
- Always carry a few sheets of paper with you, to save dashing off to the bathroom for supplies.
- If you simply cannot finish a design, send a blank check to the author, who will almost certainly help you out.

Paper Potato Chip

Everyone except the incurably health-conscious loves potato chips. Bars like them because they make the eater thirsty, there's a high profit margin, and they're not nearly as heavy as beer kegs. Drinkers love them because they go so well with beer. Few people have a decent meal before going boozing, so after an hour or so, the munchies strike and will not be denied. A bag of potato chips is just the ticket to fool your body into thinking it's getting properly fed. Better than this, you can buy a few bags and throw them around the drinking table as a perfect (and cheap) means of demonstrating your generosity. Hopefully, no-one will remember that you haven't bought a round all night.

The only food in the entire world that we eat more of than potato chips is rice. Potato chips were invented in 1853 by Native American George Crum. He was a chef, who had some of his french fries returned by a customer who wanted them sliced thinner. He obliged, only to have them once again returned as "too thick". In the end, he sliced them as thin as possible, hoping to get his revenge on the customer. The customer loved them though, and a new invention was born.

In 1920, a Londoner named Frank Smith, heard about this new way of cooking the humble potato and set up his own business in a garage. He and his wife peeled, sliced, and fried the potato pieces and put them into greaseproof bags. He then travelled around selling his new snack. Within a year he had to open up larger premises and the Smiths Crisps empire was born. He was also responsible for the idea of adding a small blue bag of salt, to allow the consumer to add their own seasoning. Many drunks managed to swallow this bag whole along with a handful of potato chips, causing several phone-calls to Ralph (see "Barf Bag").

This particular design was developed as a paper substitute for a "Poppadom" – these are served in Indian restaurants and though they look like chips, are actually made from flour. This design forms the logo of the Poppadom Society: People Out Practicing Paperfolding And Dining On Masala. At every meeting of this august and exclusive society, members must fold the logo, then hold it aloft, saying, "I fold therefore I eat". Lest you think I'm joking, pop along to www.poppadom.org.uk and read all about it!

1. Start with a square, colored side up. Apply a multiple squash-sink-reverse to the whole sheet. In other words, screw it up!

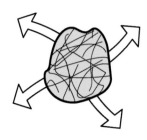

2. The result will be something like this. Unfold back to the square.

3. Repeat step 1 with a completely new set of creases.

4. Further compress the paper with care.

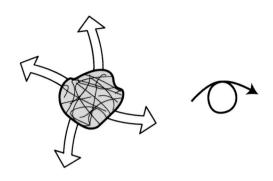

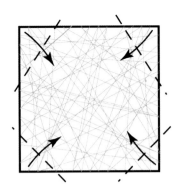

5. Unfold once more.

6. Turn to the white side and fold the corners in a little.

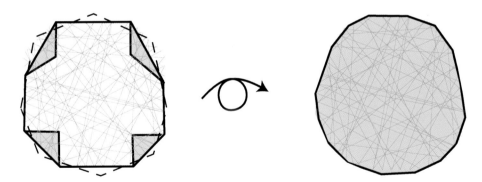

7. Fold in the new corners formed in step 6.

8. Turn over for the finished potato chip!

Origami is Good For You

Arthur Guinness established his brewery in 1759 in Dublin, Ireland. Like other cities of the time, Dublin suffered from poor sanitation and beer was routinely drunk instead of water. And they say we've made progress since then! As well as ales, Guinness brewed a beer new to Ireland containing roasted barley, which gave it a characteristic color. (Look closely and you'll see that it isn't black, but dark ruby red.) After a few glasses, it could be just about any old color. The brew was known as "porter" due to its popularity with London porters; the word "stout" was added in the 1820s to indicate a stronger, full-bodied variety. It was clearly a big hit, since the first proper advertisement for Guinness didn't appear until 1929—one hundred and seventy years later! In 1881, Guinness had an annual production of over 1 million barrels a year and, by 1914, was the world's largest brewery.

Phrases such as "Guinness is good for you" and "Guinness for potency" made the brand a household name. The artist John Gilroy produced some of the best known graphic art of the time: the Guinness Toucan first appeared in 1935. By this time the drink had become part of Anglo-Irish culture and, among other things, was recommended as a cure for anaemia and to boost the health of nursing mothers.

Beer cans first appeared in the USA in 1935, and the UK a year later. Like other major brewers, Guinness looked to improve the quality of their canned beer using every bit of new technology they could find. One such item is the "widget": a small plastic globe, which floats in the beer. Just before the can is sealed, liquid nitrogen is injected into the beer. This evaporates during the canning process pressurizing the can. When the can is opened, the pressure drops suddenly and the nitrogen escapes through a small hole in the widget, causing it to spin through the beer, frothing it up and creating the same creamy head that you expect on a glass poured from a tap... So next time the topic surfaces in a quiz, you'll be able to impress everyone.

This design by Alex Bateman lends itself to variations—a full pint, half full, empty, and, with some thought, even a "Guinness on the Titanic". The average drunk will think he is seeing a glass from ten yards away.

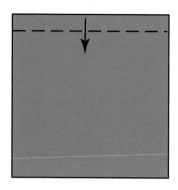

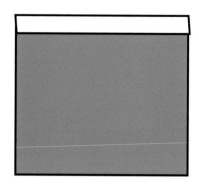

1. Start with a square, colored side up. Fold a small flap down at the top.

2. This is the result. Turn the paper over.

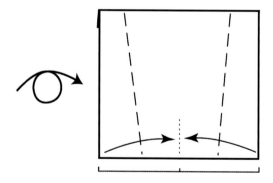

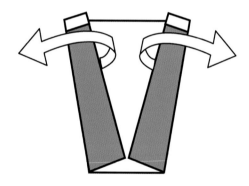

3. Fold both lower corners to an imaginary center crease, slightly up from the lower edge.

4. Like this. Unfold both flaps.

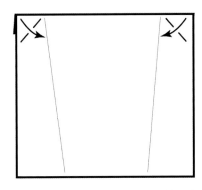 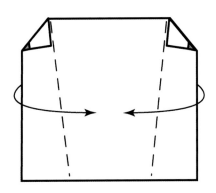

5. Fold the top corners over to lie along the creases made in step 4.

6. Re-fold the sides inwards.

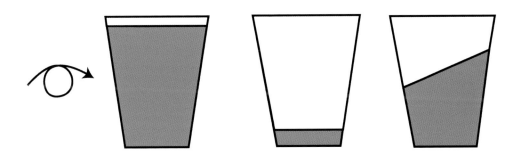

7. Turn over for the completed "full" glass.
See if you can adapt the design to create an empty glass
and the half-full "Titanic" glass!

Emergency Beer Glass

There have been many books written about how the bar forms an epicenter for the social interaction of today's homogenous multi-culture, but we all know that really, a bar is where you swig beer. In large quantities. Failing that, you might be into the spirit world. Worst case scenario, you're either sober or driving, in which case I recommend tea, or hot chocolate, if it's cold outside. However, I digress—the bar is for drinking. So how does the origami drinker convey the nectar of the gods to their throat?

In the ancient days, cavemen would form a cup with their hands. The more clever ones might have formed a leaf into a temporary drinking vessel (perhaps a primitive form of origami!). Pottery opened up a whole new world and soon became the favorite for cup makers. In northern Belize, an unwashed 2,600-year-old Mayan ceramic cup has been found to contain cocoa powder. This establishes two important facts: a) our chocolate addiction has lasted for a very long time and b) the Mayans didn't do the dishes.

Serious drinkers will have a stein of their own. The word is German in origin (from "Steingut", meaning stone goods). They are large mugs (up to 8.4 gallons!) used specifically for drinking beer. They are variously made from porcelain, stoneware, wood, pewter, crystal, earthenware, silver, or glass. Their standard form is with a handle and a hinged lid—the bubonic plague and various plagues of flies caused Germany to establish laws requiring drinking cups to be covered up for sanitary purposes. They are also frequently decorated in a Gothic style, due to their 14th century European origins.

This origami cup is a traditional design that is known around the world. The U. S. marines are taught how to fold it so they can rustle one up in the jungle if the need arises. If you ever apply to join the marines, they will be so impressed if you already know this fold!

Unless the paper is very thin, it can be recycled several times. There is also the added excitement of not knowing exactly when the bottom will tear, with obvious consequences.

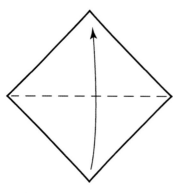

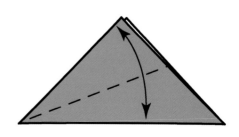

1. Start with a square, colored side down. Fold in half from corner to opposite corner.

2. Fold the top-left edge to meet the bottom edge, crease and unfold.

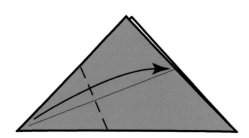

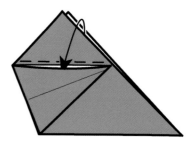

3. Fold the left-hand corner to meet the end of the crease.

4. Fold the first triangular layer of paper all the way into the pocket and flatten.

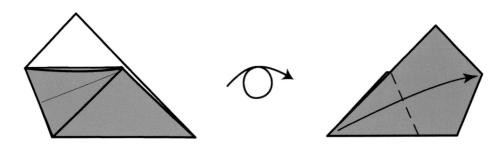

5. This is the result. Turn the paper over.

6. Fold the left-hand corner to meet the opposite corner.

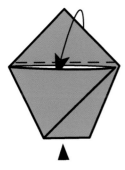

7. Tuck the flap into the pocket as in step 4. Open the cup by pressing gently at the base.

8. Complete. Just add beer.

Peanut Dish

The most important thing to know about peanuts is that they aren't nuts at all, but legumes—part of the pea family. They are also known as "groundnuts", since they actually grow underground. They are highly versatile culinary items, and so is their tastiest product, peanut butter.

Peanuts have played a part in the lives of many men, but none more so than George Washington Carver. Born a slave in 1860, he was adopted and grew to become a respected botanist who encouraged growth of crops other than cotton, including the peanut. He took this humble nut and came up with over 300 products including laundry soap, relish, soil conditioner, wall boards, washing powder, wood filler, shoe polish, shaving cream, meatloaf, insecticide, toothpaste, coffee, and a cure for both bronchitis and venereal disease.

One of the best known uses of the peanut is to make peanut butter. In fact half of all edible peanuts produced in America are used to make peanut butter. Americans love peanuts so much that National Peanut Week was launched in 1941 and, since 1974, March has been designated as National Peanut Month. An Australian inventor has reputedly invented a car that runs using peanut butter.

Grinding your own couldn't be simpler and certainly couldn't be tastier. It makes rich, thick butter that cements your tongue to your palate like no other. Health conscious peanut fans can regulate the amount of rock salt added to the mix.

Nuts are, of course, a vital part of bar snacks, along with potato chips and pretzels. Added to that, on average, is the urine of at least eleven unwashed hands, both male and female. The best way to avoid this problem is to fold your own nut tray, buy your own nuts and fill it yourself. If people want some, insist on pouring them into their hands and explain you are doing this because they may have urine on their hands. It's a great pick up line at parties!

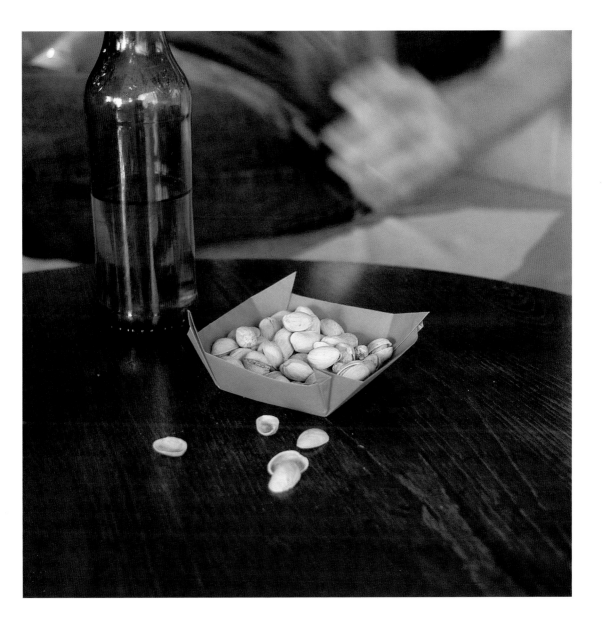

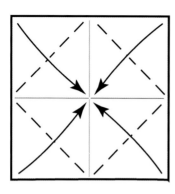
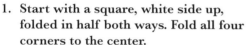

1. Start with a square, white side up, folded in half both ways. Fold all four corners to the center.

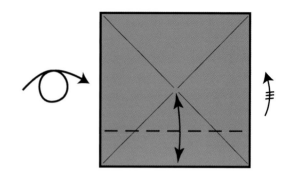

2. Turn the paper over and fold each edge to the center, crease and unfold.

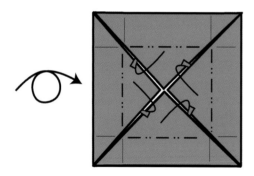

3. Turn over once more and tuck the four flaps inside.

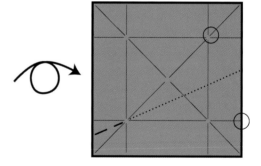

4. Turn back over. Fold the paper through the lower-left intersection, so that the two circled points meet (see next picture).

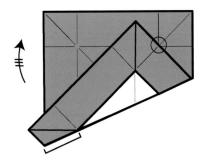

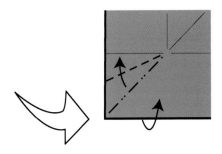

5. Like this. Crease only where shown. Repeat on the other three sides.

6. Unfold the last crease and reform it as shown. The dish becomes 3D.

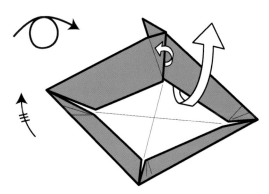

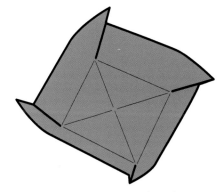

7. Look underneath and ease out some paper so that it traps the fold made in the last step. Repeat all round.

8. Turn over for the completed tray.

Cunning Disguise Kit

Most people in loving relationships have established reasonably clear ground rules for drinking schedules, in-law visits (one shot of whisky before arrival, none during, lots afterwards), The Home Shopping Network vs. Football on TV and so on. However, there comes a time in everyone's life when they simply must slip away from the stresses of everyday life—and their partner—for a visit to their local bar. Such a visit often necessitates going without a partner's knowledge, much less their consent.

So, picture the scene. You're sitting on your favorite barstool, sipping your favorite brew, when the barman says, "Hey, isn't that your wife/husband/girlfriend/boyfriend?" Panic sets in as you try to think of some reasonable excuse as to why you didn't say where you were going. As Aldous Huxley once said, "Several excuses are always less convincing than one". So sort yourself out a good one, such as the young lady who was pulled over for not wearing her seatbelt. In court, she explained that she was an exotic dancer and the seatbelt pinched her nipple rings in a painful fashion. She even offered to show the judge, but he gave her a fine anyway.

However, how much better it would be if your partner didn't even know you were there in the first place? All you need is the Bar Origami Cunning Disguise Kit. This consists of two parts: the moustache and the sunglasses. Men have an unfair advantage here: they can wear both parts of a disguise. Some women may have to make do without the sunglasses. In order to be convincing, you should have a genuine Moustache Stein —an ancient German drinking vessel of indeterminate origin with a special "lip" to keep the froth from your moustache. You can pick these up on Ebay from time to time.

Have both items pre-folded and stored safely inside your jacket pocket. Try to use paper of a suitable color, or the effect will be reversed. When the barman gives you the word, quickly and quietly slip your nose inside the moustache and don the sunglasses. Slouch down in the chair, stick out your lower jaw in true Kirk Douglas style and pick your nose. Unless this is your usually relaxing posture, the combination will render you virtually invisible to your partner.

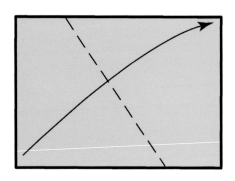

1. For the sunglasses, start with a piece of paper (standard business paper size) colored side up. Fold bottom-left to top-right corner.

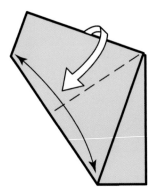

2. Fold the two corners shown to meet each other, crease and unfold completely.

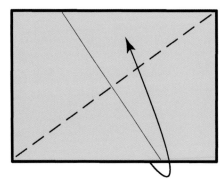

3. Fold over on the crease made in the last step.

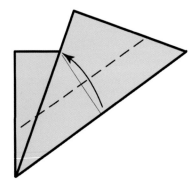

4. Fold one end of the crease to meet the other end.

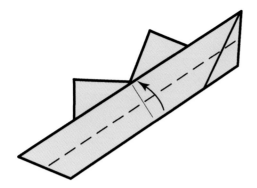

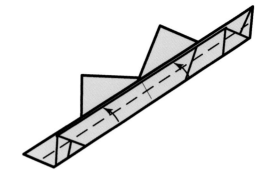

5. Fold the strip in half.

6. And in half again.

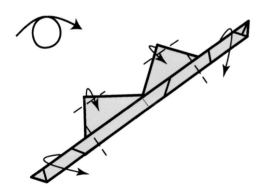

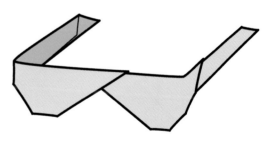

7. Fold the tips of the two triangles over to round them. Shape the thin strips to fit your ears.

8. Ready for use.

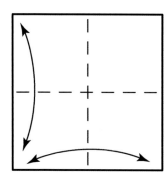 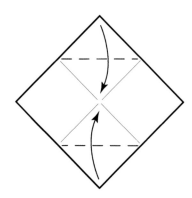

1. For the moustache, start with a square, white side up. Fold both sides to the opposite side, crease and unfold.

2. Fold two opposite corners to the center.

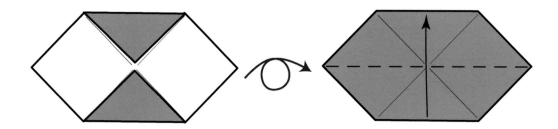

3. Like this. Turn the paper over.

4. Take the lower folded edge to meet the opposite edge.

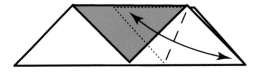

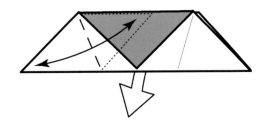

5. Fold the right-hand raw edges over to lie along the lower edge. Crease and unfold.

6. Repeat on the left-hand side, then unfold the layer from behind.

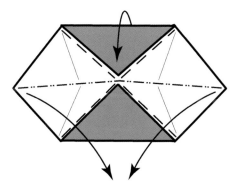

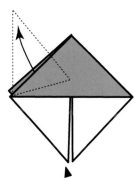

7. Use the creases shown to collapse the paper. No new creases are added.

8. This is the result. Reverse fold one of the points upwards using the crease made in step 5.

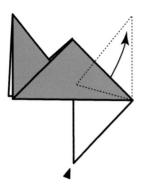

9. Repeat on the other side.

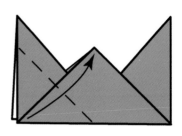

10. Fold the lower-left corner to the central top corner.

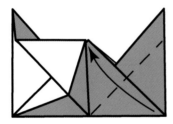

11. Repeat on the right-hand side.

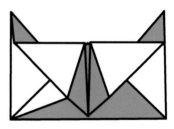

12. This is the result. Turn the paper over.

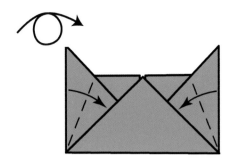

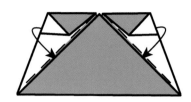

13. Fold both vertical edges to lie along the edges of the triangular flap.

14. Fold them over again, then tuck them into the pockets. Turn the paper over.

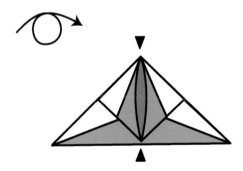

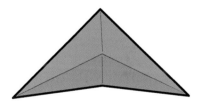

15. Press gently at the top and bottom to open a small pocket. Shape the front of the moustache. Pop your nose into the pocket!

16. Complete.

Frog Olympics

In any random group of office workers, you'll find an average of four out of every seven have business cards. They're also usually eager to give them away, in the hope of juicy business deals coming their way. (Plus, it makes them feel important). As a Bar Origamist, you can take advantage of their generosity by converting their cards into frogs, thus winning new friends and influencing people.

If you want to be Top Frog, you gotta jump. As the frog-jumping capital of the world, California is the place to hop along to. Due to a legal provision, it is illegal to take frogs from the wild, but there is a 1957 provision in the Fish and Game Code which allows it for the specific purposes of frog-jumping contests (provided you return them later). The current triple jump champ is Rosie the Ribbitter, who made a distance of twenty-one feet 5¾ inches in 1986.

Whatever you do, don't confuse frogs and toads. Certainly not in front of enthusiasts, when it can lead to arguments, warts, or worse. The best way to tell them apart is to put them in a pond and wait until breeding time. Frogs lays clusters of eggs, whereas toads lay strings.

The true monster of the batrachian world is the cane toad, *Bufo marinus*. This was introduced to Australia by the sugar cane industry in order to control pests of sugar cane. One hundred and one toads (why that number? I have no idea!) arrived in North Queensland in June 1935. Within six months there were over 60,000 hopping about. Their success was due to both their inherent nastiness—cane toads have glands on their heads filled with highly toxic venom, enough to kill a dog within fifteen minutes of eating one; their ability to eat almost anything, including bacon, mice, rabbits, and small cats; and the fact that they also lay 40,000 eggs each at a time!

Frogs are natural gymnasts and their paper brethren share this ability. After a few drinks, what better activity to organize than your very own Frog Olympics? You can devise categories of your own, but to start with, how about the trio of long jump, high jump, and triple jump? Playing frogliwinks with glasses of whisky is also equally entertaining.

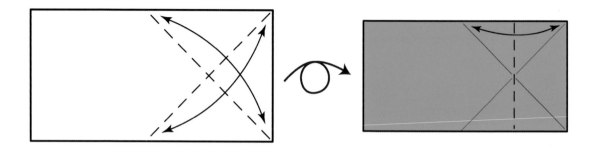

1. Start with a business card. Fold a short edge to one long edge, then the other.

2. Turn the paper over. Fold the short edge so the corners meet the ends of the creases. Crease and unfold.

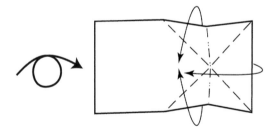

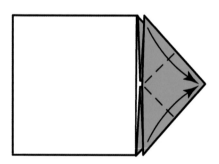

3. Turn the paper over. Use the creases shown to collapse the paper into a triangular flap.

4. Fold both flaps over so they are just outside the end corner.

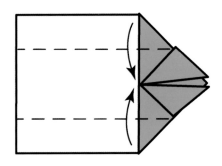

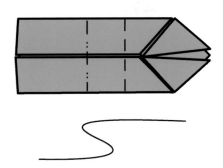

5. Like this. Fold the longer edges in to meet (more or less) in the center.

6. Carefully fold the body into an S-shape. Do NOT make firm creases!

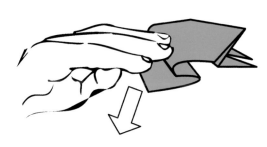

7. Gently press down on the back of the body and slip your finger quickly backwards. You'll need to work on this technique.

Basketball

Basketball was invented in 1891 by a Canadian physical education instructor called James Naismith. The aim was to provide indoor exercise and competition for his students between the end of the football season and the start of the baseball season. Over the years, it has developed a peculiar attraction for players with unusual names. Try doing a commentary on a team including Krzyzewsky, Gheorghe, Gugliotta, Marciulionis, Jacikevicius, Ilgauskas, and Szczerbiak!

Patient and dedicated research has uncovered several links between basketball and sex: the key to both is controlled ball movement. If you need a break, you can call a time out. If the watching talent scouts like your performance, you turn professional. You always try to score within 24 seconds and you know you are done when the horn sounds. If that isn't impressive enough, there is a coach shouting at you to "take it to the hole" and if you are going nowhere, you can pass so that your friend can score.

There are dangers to the game though. In 1946, during Boston Celtics v. Chicago Stags, a certain Chuck Conners dunked the ball so hard that it broke the backboard, which then toppled on to him and put him in hospital. During another game, Wiley Peck of Mississippi State tried to impress everyone with how hard he could dunk the ball. He slammed it so hard it rebounded into his face and knocked him unconscious for eight minutes!

When a foul is committed, the "fouled" player gets a number of "free throws", where he can try to score with only the jeering of the crowd to put him off. This origami model allows you to hold your own free throws.

The important thing to remember is that wherever you throw from, you mustn't knock the hoop over. If your players are excessively inebriated, you might relax this rule and tape the hoop to a wall somewhere.

Don't forget, the instructions for making the ball are contained in the first few steps of the "Paper Potato Chip".

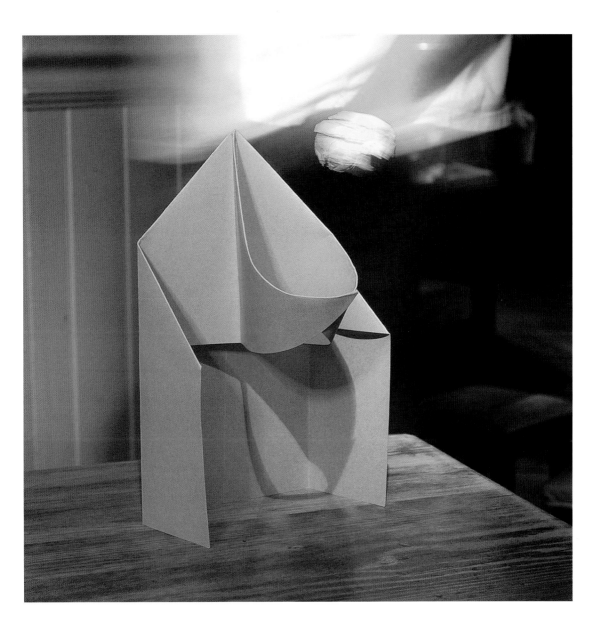

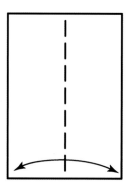

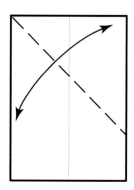

1. Start with a rectangle of paper (standard business paper). Fold in half, long edge to long edge.

2. Fold the top-right corner to meet the vertical left-hand side.

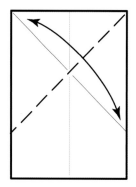

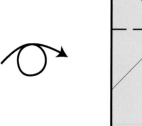

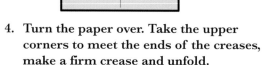

3. Repeat the fold to the other side.

4. Turn the paper over. Take the upper corners to meet the ends of the creases, make a firm crease and unfold.

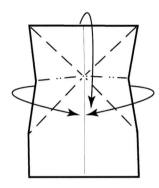

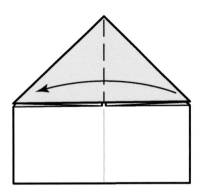

5. Turn the paper back over. Using the creases shown, carefully flatten the paper down into a triangle.

6. Fold the upper right-hand flap to the left.

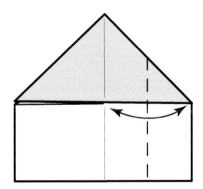

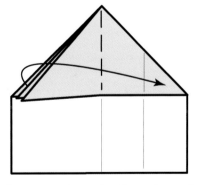

7. Fold the right-hand vertical edge to the center, crease and unfold.

8. Swing two triangular flaps from the left to the right.

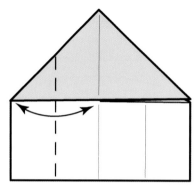

9. Repeat step 7 on the left-hand side.

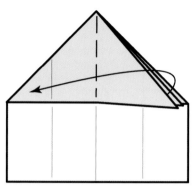

10. Fold a single flap from the right over to the left.

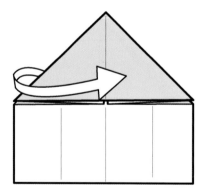

11. Start to curl the upper left-hand flap round to the right. Don't crease it.

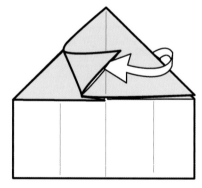

12. Repeat with the right-hand flap and feed one inside the other.

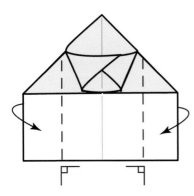

13. Fold the outer flaps in at right angles to form the stand.

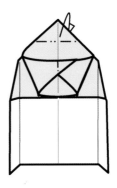

14. You can fold the top point behind to add strength, if you like.

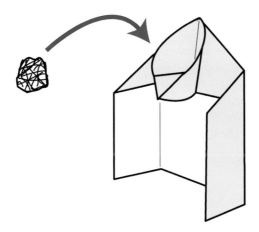

15. Complete.

Sumo Wrestlers

Sumo has its origins in the Shinto religion of Japan. Sumo bouts were dedicated to the gods in return for a good harvest. A sumo match, or *basho*, has changed little over the centuries and is rich in ceremonial acts. From the moment the wrestlers throw salt into the ring to purify it spiritually, they are following a well-established ritual. The referee (*gyoji*) wears a fancy kimono and a strange hat. After a series of opening rituals, the contest begins.

The object of sumo wrestling is to push, pull, throw, or otherwise persuade your opponent to leave the ring (known as a *dohyo*); your opponent also loses if anything other than his feet touches the playing surface. There are no weight categories, but body mass coupled with a low center of gravity is a distinct advantage, so every sumo wrestler's ambition is to pile on those pounds in order to have an advantage. In order to do this, they eat rice, bacon, and small animals between bouts.

There are seventy ways of beating an opponent, including *uwatenage* (overarm throw) and *shitatenage* (underarm throw), but few methods of attack are banned. Wrestlers wear a silk belt (*mawashi*) which can be pulled up nice and tight by an opponent—this technique is known as *yorikiri*, which roughly translates as "Phew, that makes my eyes water!". Wrestlers may trip or slap or fart or snarl nastily, but eye-gouging, hair-pulling, and crotch poking are not permitted and will result in forfeiting the bout.

Sumo is big on ranking. The upper division wrestlers (*rikishi*) fight fifteen bouts in each of the six tournaments per year, while the lower divisions fight seven bouts. Promotions and demotions depend on the results. Each win beyond a scrape-through record of eight wins and seven losses improves a wrestler's ranking. A Grand Champion (*Yokozuna*) is expected to win 13–2 or better, or they lose face and generally retire. Although almost exclusively a Japanese sport, in 1993 a Hawaiian fighting under the name Akebono was promoted to Yokozuna, the first time a non-Japanese achieved the top rank.

Our little paper wrestlers should be carefully lined up facing each other in a suitable ring. You then bang and tilt the table in order to upset your opponent whilst keeping your player's feet firmly on the ground.

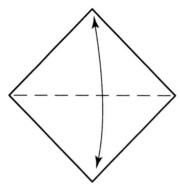

1. Start with a square, colored side down. Fold in half from corner to opposite corner, then unfold.

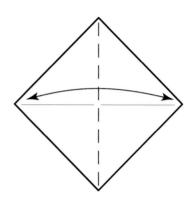

2. Add the other diagonal.

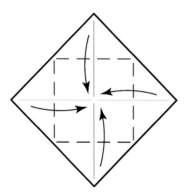

3. Fold all four corners to the center of the paper.

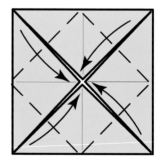

4. Once again, fold four corners to the center.

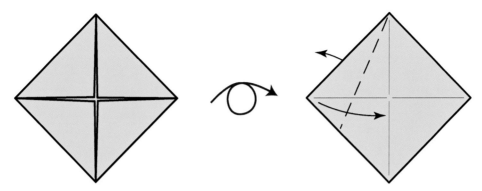

5. This is the result. Turn the paper over.

6. Fold the upper-left edge in to the center crease, letting the flap underneath flip out.

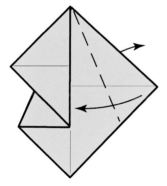

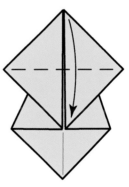

7. Like this. Repeat on the other side.

8. Now fold the upper square in half.

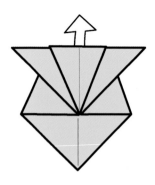

9. Allow a small triangle of paper to pop up from behind.

10. Turn the paper over and fold the lower triangular flap upwards.

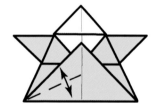
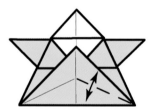

11. Fold the upper-left edge of the triangle to meet the lower edge.

12. Repeat on the right-hand side.

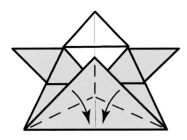

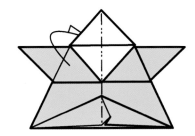

13. Fold both these creases in at the same time, forming a small point in the center.

14. Fold the model in half behind using the vertical center crease.

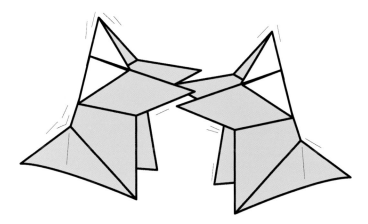

15. Make two, find a suitable venue and get wrestling!

Thirsty Bird

Unlikely as it seems, birds can develop a taste for alcohol. Not that they can get a hold of it easily, unless they live near bars. Those that do are notorious for dropping by to siphon off your whisky as you watch the sun set. A magpie known locally as Joe, lived in the country town of Matlock Bath in Derbyshire, England. He was so adept at stealing drinks from the local pub, which was appropriately called *The Fishpond*, that he was officially barred from flying over or landing near the premises. The landlord, an otherwise friendly character named Jib (on account of his impressive nose), would spend many hours of the day running outside to enforce the legislation. After a few wild pot-shots with his air rifle, the bird eventually got the message and departed for pastures (and presumably pubs) anew.

Other critters are equally fond of the occasional drink. Dogs, rats, and mice have all been known to imbibe, given half a chance. Slugs and snails have an especial fondness of the amber nectar and this is put to good use by organic gardeners. Avoiding chemicals and poisons, they bury a glass of beer in the garden. The snails, scenting the aroma from over twenty yards away, hurry to take advantage, but slip in and drown. You can rid yourself of 10–15 a night using this process with the bonus that they die happy. Since recent legislation forbids "excessive cruelty" to all creatures large and small (even slugs) this is a very useful means of lowering your resident mollusk population. When hauled before the local magistrate, you can claim that you were holding a party in your yard and therefore not responsible for the behavior of drunken mollusks.

This design will probably take more practice to fold properly than the other designs in this book, but it is well worth it. By the time you have made three, you should be able to add some life and poise into the model, so that it looks realistic and impressive. The designer is a highly respected Japanese origami master named Kunihiko Kasahara, who, by happy coincidence, isn't averse to the occasional drink himself. You should seek out some of the 120 plus books he has written in order to enjoy his work more fully.

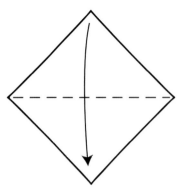
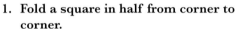

1. Fold a square in half from corner to corner.

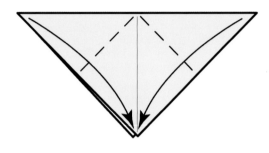

2. Fold the outside corners to the lower corner.

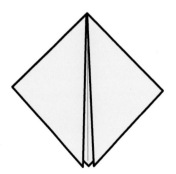

3. Like this. Turn the paper over.

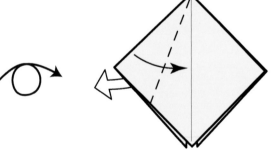

4. Fold the upper-left edge to the vertical crease, allowing the paper to flip out from behind.

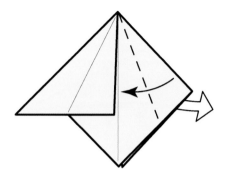

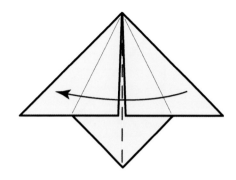

5. Like this. Repeat on the right-hand side.

6. Fold the paper in half from right to left.

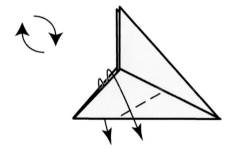

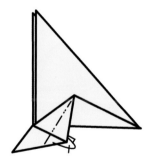

7. Rotate to this postition. Open the paper out and wrap it around (an outside reverse) on the crease shown.

8. Fold part of the tail inside on either side.

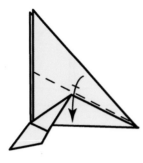

9. Fold both wings downwards.

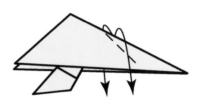

10. Make another outside reverse fold to form the head.

11. Fold the tip of the head in and out to form a beak.

12. This is the result.

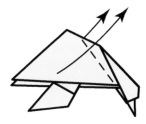

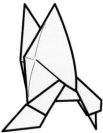

13. Fold the wings up on a crease that doesn't meet the outside edge. This makes the wings 3D. Fold carefully!

14. This is the result.

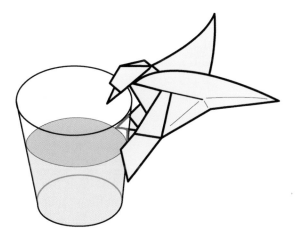

15. After all that hard work, the bird is ready for a drink.

Emergency Date

Most human beings are gregarious by nature. In plain language, they like company. Going to a bar simply to sit in a corner and drink by yourself isn't many people's idea of fun. This is why "boys" or "girls" nights out are so popular—if twelve of you agree to meet for a drink, there's every chance most will make it and you're not alone. Dating is a much less assured good time—there's always the chance you'll be left in the lurch, until now!

This cute little puppy is easy to fold and will never let you down. You can talk with it all night (as long as you don't mind the puzzled stares from other tables) and you simply cannot find a less expensive date!

Like their owners, dogs can develop a taste for booze and follow them into bars. Here, they look "cute" and people obligingly give them chips, peanuts, and the occasional saucer of beer. This leads to dogs that are first of all merry, then become very sad and finally stagger off to find somewhere to sleep.

In Tennessee, workers at an animal shelter were called upon to take a dog from the local slammer. Both the dog and its owner had too much to drink and were locked up. The dog, a cocker spaniel, was described as "wobbly, with bloodshot eyes," said one witness. A report was received from a restaurant about a woman with a small dog, both of whom appeared to be intoxicated and one of whom was swearing, according to the police report. The woman left the restaurant and was apprehended along with her dog.

The woman was charged with public intoxication and fined. The dog was released to the shelter on Saturday, but not before being treated for a hangover (a real case of "hair of the dog"). Workers said the dog was "laid out" the next day, until they gave it an aspirin. After this, it "pepped up and became friendly."

This little origami pooch also has a talent for sniffing things out. Balance his head carefully so it can swing from side to side. Then take a plastic comb (or ruler) and rub it on your sweater or hair, to charge it with static electricity. Move the comb near to the dog's nose and he will turn his head towards it!

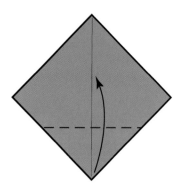

1. For the body, start with a square, colored side up, with a diagonal crease. Fold over about one third along the diagonal.

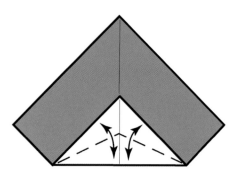

2. Fold each upper edge of the triangular flap to the lower edge, crease and return.

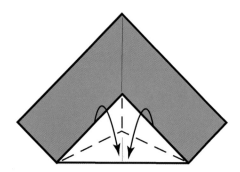

3. Put both creases in together, pinching the flap into a point.

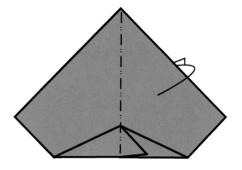

4. Fold the right-hand half of the model behind.

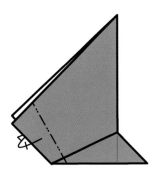

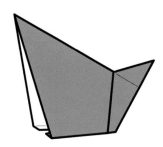

5. Fold a flap behind on both sides (see next diagram for guidance).

6. Rotate to this position. The body is complete.

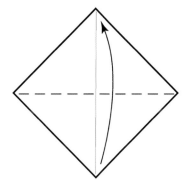

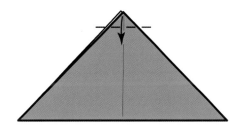

1. For the head, start with a square (the same size as the body), white side up, with a diagonal crease. Fold in half on the other diagonal.

2. Fold over both layers to form the nose.

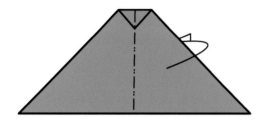

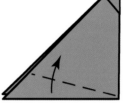

3. Fold the head in half underneath.

4. Fold an ear over.

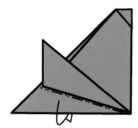

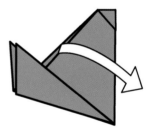

5. And the other ear.

6. Open the head from underneath.

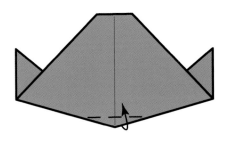

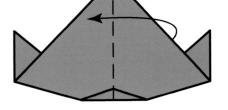

7. Fold over a small corner.

8. Refold the head in half.

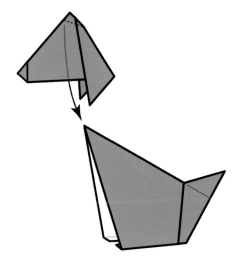

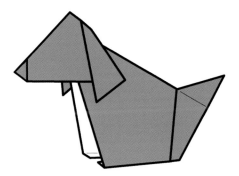

9. Carefully balance the head onto the body.

10. Complete.

"It's Your Round" Butterfly

Butterflies and beer? Shurely shome mishtake. However, dear reader, a little patience and all will be revealed. Spending a night with good friends, imbibing a drink is a fine way to pass the night. However, there are always a lot of undercover calculations going on to work out who should buy the first round. The aim of the process is to ensure if anyone pays for more rounds than the others, it isn't going to be you. The following formula has been worked out by members of the British Origami Gourmet Society (BOGS) to help solve the problem.

$$((CT - OT) - (T \times enp) / (AA \times \pi)) / p)$$
$$\times (d / (nobs \times absiq)$$

Where CT = closing time, OT = opening time, T = time taken to use the bathroom, enp = estimated number of drinks, AA = average age of your party, π = 3.142, the typical number of treats consumed during the night, p = the number of people in your party, d = total number of drinkers expected in the bar that night, nobs = number of bar staff, absiq = average bar staff IQ. A more accurate answer is obtained by differentially integrating a factor based on the average decibel noise level within 1.3 feet of the bar. So my friend Gareth tells me.

So where does the butterfly come in? Well, it's based on the premise that your friends won't be familiar with this calculation and will say, "Let's toss for it." Schoolboy jokes aside, there is an origami alternative to tossing. Fold the butterfly, write the name of one potential round-buyer on one side, the next on the other side. Launch the butterfly and let it flutter realistically to the floor. The name on the side that lands face up is entered into the next round. Repeat the process with pairs of people until the first group is eliminated, then start again with the first two in the next round. Eventually, you'll get down to the last pair, the winner of which does *not* buy the first round. The process is then repeated with the losers.

While this is going on, you whip out your calculator and perform the necessary math. If you determine that you should get the first round, interrupt the proceedings with a cry of "Oh okay, I'll buy them...". There may be simpler means of using this "yes or no" design, but they're not nearly so much fun.

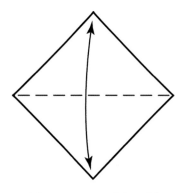

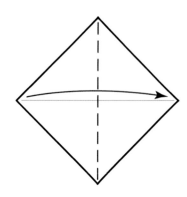

1. Start with a square, white side up,
   crease and unfold a diagonal crease.

2. Fold in half from left to right.

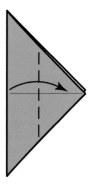

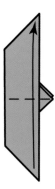

3. Take the folded edge over, leaving a
   slight gap on the right.

4. Fold in half from bottom to top.

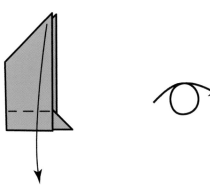

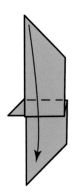

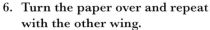

5. Fold a wing down level with the back of the head.

6. Turn the paper over and repeat with the other wing.

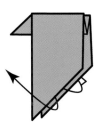

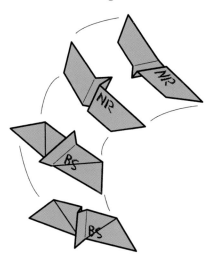

7. Fold both wings out half way.

8. Throw high in the air and keep your fingers crossed!

Drunkeness Indicator

According to the dictionary, drunkenness is "a temporary state resulting from excessive alcohol consumption". What an inadequate description! It makes no reference to the fact that, whilst drunk, you can appeal to members of the opposite sex, make new friends, discover unknown resources of wit and wisdom, lose all your inhibitions about nakedness, eat your lunch in reverse and even fly for short distances. Moreover, I would argue that you can achieve all this with merely "adequate" consumption.

The difference between "adequate" and "excessive" is hard to quantify, and varies with the individual and the circumstances in which they drink. Arriving late to a night out encourages a faster than normal acceleration towards inebriation. Conversely, some nights can be so dull that you can consume far more than your normal limit without side effects.

Back to our definition—"a temporary state": this too is not always the case. There are some who seem to be in a permanent state of stupefaction. They may just have a real talent for it, or they may be sneaking in a shooter or two to help them through the day.

However, as most drinkers will testify, your body normally realizes when you're overly drunk and will encourage you to lie down and remain in this position for several hours.

It's a good thing that drunkenness doesn't last, since it is usually followed by various unpleasant side effects. Of these, loss of bladder control and the inability to walk in a straight line are the least of your worries. The greatest evil by far is the dreaded "spins": you are lying on your bed, eyes closed and the room begins to spin. A curiously detached part of your bleary intellect tells you that the bed isn't moving, nor is your body, but your senses tell you that you are sinking through the mattress and rotating at the same time. You may soon be calling for Ralph (*see* Barf-Bag).

This superb model by Max Hulme is a good measure of a person's drunkenness. Pretend to thread an invisible needle through the point, then gently pull the "thread" up and down, simultaneously making the pointer rise and fall by squeezing the base. If they swear they can see the thread, they're probably drunk. If you can see it, you're paralytic.

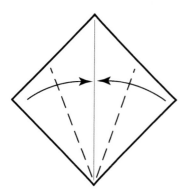

1. Start with a square, white side up, with a diagonal crease. Fold opposite sides to lie on the crease.

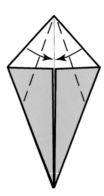

2. Fold the remaining raw edges in as well.

3. Fold the lowest edges in to the center.

4. Fold the upper triangular flap down.

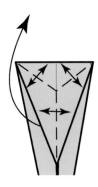

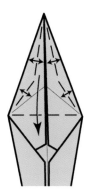

5. Make a bisecting crease at each corner of the upper triangular flap, then unfold the flap upwards.

6. Fold the outside edges in to meet the center or the nearest crease, then fold the flap down again.

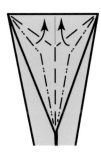

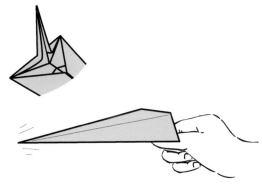

7. Reform the creases shown, but only enough to form a flap you can hold—it should stay 3D.

8. A bit like this. Gently test the mechanism—a subtle squeeze should cause the tip to rise. Ensure that your victim cannot see your fingers moving.

Firecracker

Sound is a wonderful thing. If you like it, it's called music. If you don't, it's called noise. One man's Chopin is another's System Of A Down (note for old fogies, the latter are a popular rock band). Our ears are capable of detecting an amazing range of sound levels, which we measure in decibels (DBs for short). Here are some examples:

- Space Shuttle taking off (180DB): Irreversible hearing loss
- Mother-in-law shouting (140DB): Painfully loud
- Heavy metal rock concert (110DB): Extremely loud
- Boom box on shoulder (90DB): Very annoying
- Cow mooing from 2 feet away (80DB): Annoying
- Raccoons making love (60DB): Intrusive
- Eating potato chip (50 DB): Quiet
- Store clerk shouting "You've forgotten your change" (20DB): Almost inaudible
- Ant farting (10DB): Silent, but deadly

However, our ability to detect sound is undermined somewhat by our inability to detect where the sound came from. This allows sneaky farters to unleash their best baked bean specials and, providing they can keep a straight face, get away with it. We have easily recognizable beeping alarms built into our cell phones, yet when they go off, we spend ten minutes trying to figure out which corner of the room they might be hiding in.

So where does our origami firecracker come in this pantheon of sound? It depends on a) the paper and b) your technique. The paper should be crisp and strong, but not too heavy. 6 x 8-inch paper will pop, 8 x 11-inch will bang and 11 x 17-inch, if it survives, will deafen anyone with 3 feet. Do watch out for elderly folk when you feel like a good explosion.

Technique wise, in order to get the loudest possible explosion, you need to pull the firecracker straight down rather than in an arc. After a while, they do get tired and finally rip, so make sure you keep a few spares handy to practice with.

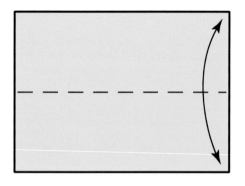

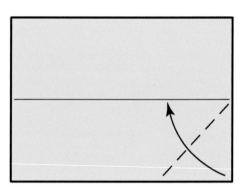

1. Start with a large rectangle of paper of tough-ish paper. Fold this in half, crease and unfold.

2. Fold a corner to the center crease.

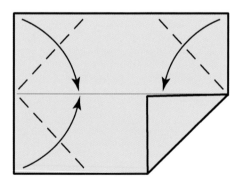

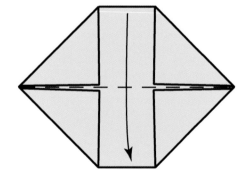

3. Repeat with the three other corners.

4. Fold the paper in half, top to bottom.

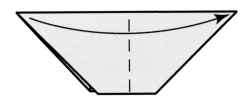

5. Fold in half from left to right.

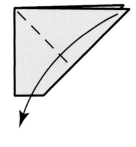

6. Fold the upper flap down at a 45° angle.

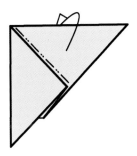

7. Repeat with the flap underneath.

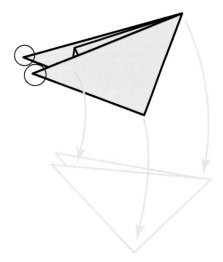

8. Hold by the two points, with the point of the triangle facing down. Hold it high in the air, then pull the paper straight down, as fast as possible.

Peanut Catapult

Catapults were a form of field artillery first used by the Ancient Greeks. The word catapult comes from the Greek words *kata* (downward) and *pultos* (referring to a small circular shield carried in battle). Later on came the ballista and trebuchet. The ballista was propelled by using thick ropes to create tension for the moving arm of the catapult. This was used to launch sheep and small cows at a castle. The trebuchet used heavy weights and a sling to propel dead people inside the castle.

Back in the days when schoolboys in England had to learn Latin, "catties" were a favorite weapon of choice. They were used to launch erasers, chalk, dead rats, and anything else found in a jacket pocket. Ammunition needs to be carefully considered, to ensure no real damage is sustained. Screwed up balls of paper and grapes are fine, but the humble peanut is the perfect combination of size and weight. What's more, you can buy packets of ammunition at every bar. The dry roasted variety tend to be more accurate than salted, because the granules of salt cause turbulence during flight.

This design has been adapted from an idea by the great Japanese folder, Satoshi Kamiya, and is capable of projecting a peanut with great accuracy, over a great distance. Better than that, it's a kind of origami "stealth" weapon, since you can fire it with minimal hand movement. This, of course, allows you to launch a series of attacks over twenty minutes, with the victim completely unable to work out where the darn things are coming from.

In order to hit your target accurately, you should have the open face of the cup facing away from you, then (in the words of a Zen philosopher) "Be the peanut". Focus on it and let it flow in you and around you. Visualize your target. See no other people. Finally snap your hands apart as rapidly as you can. Keep staring at a picture on the wall and give no outwards sign anything has happened. Pray to whatever gods you worship that it doesn't land in the cleavage of the girlfriend of a 6' 2" Conan the Beerbarian.

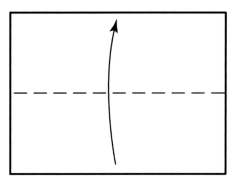

1. Start with a rectangle of paper, A4 or A5, for example. Fold one long edge to meet the other.

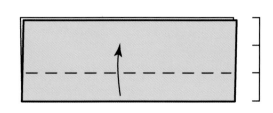

2. Fold over about one third of the height.

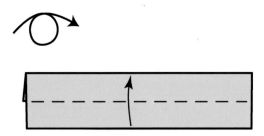

3. Turn the paper over, then fold it in half.

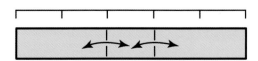

4. Make two valley creases to outline the central part of the paper, around about one fifth of the total length.

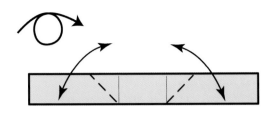 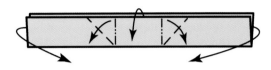

5. Turn the paper over. Make two valley creases at 45° to the vertical.

6. Fold either side towards each other, opening out a small pocket.

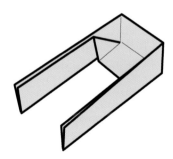 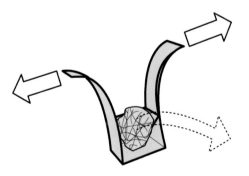

7. Like this.

8. Hold the paper as shown, pop your ammo in and snap the sides rapidly apart.

Beer Bomb

This is the well-known "waterbomb". I first learned this design as a schoolboy, when some of my more disgusting colleagues (stand up "Spewy" Eason) filled them "the quick way" with no need for a tap, or indeed, for water. We won't dwell on that. It's the perfect weapon—quickly assembled, highly effective, non-lethal and will seriously annoy people. Where else can you get so many benefits for free?

As a design, it has quite a long history, certainly since the 17th century. It is shown in a plate from *Li Tre Trattati*, by Mattia Giegere, which was published in Italy in 1639. More of this fascinating historical data, plus much more besides, can be found in the "theory" section of the British Origami Society website.

In the context of this book, we advise filling your bomb with beer—the wetter the better. Reassure yourself that the hurling of these "gifts" in the general direction of people's heads isn't entirely a bad thing. Beer has in fact been used as a successful shampoo since the 14th century. The following lines appear in Chaucer's immortal "Canterbury Tales";

A millere was ther dwellynge many a day;
As any pecok he was proud and gay.
Pipen he koude and fisshe, and droonke beere,
And ysed it eek for to wayshe his hare

There's a bit of a knack to getting maximum results from your weapon. Tearing a small amount of paper from the opening before inflating it creates a larger opening through which to carefully load it. Once charged, hold it in your hand for around a minute (depending on the type of paper)—you have to judge when the paper is soaked through, but still strong enough to be launched.

The idea is for the paper to be so saturated it literally explodes on contact. In order to hit your target accurately, you should release it using the technique employed by shot putters. Nestle it into your neck, then launch in a swift but steady movement. As with the Peanut Catapult, pray that it doesn't land on the beautifully conditioned hair of anyone larger than yourself.

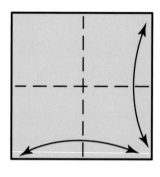 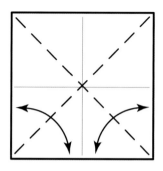

1. **Start with a square, colored side upwards. Fold from side to opposite side both ways.**

2. **Turn the paper over and add diagonals.**

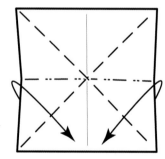 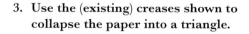 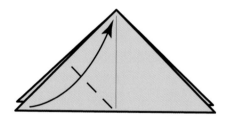

3. **Use the (existing) creases shown to collapse the paper into a triangle.**

4. **Fold the lower-left corner (upper layer only) to the top corner.**

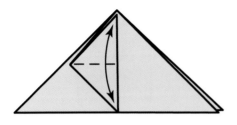

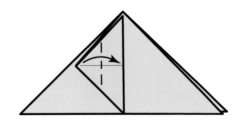

5. Fold the top corner to the bottom, crease and unfold.

6. Now fold the left corner to the center.

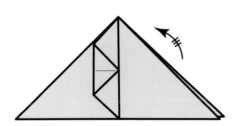

7. Repeat the last three steps on the other three flaps.

8. Fold the top-left corner to the center.

9. Fold the triangular flap over the folded edge, crease and unfold.

10. Now tuck the same flap neatly into the little pocket.

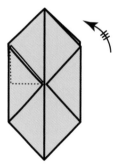

11. Repeat the last three steps on the other three flaps.

12. Fold the top corner to the center, crease and unfold.

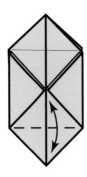

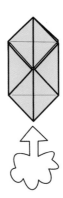

13. Do the same with the lower corner. To make filling easier, tear or cut off a small bit of the point.

14. In the center of the lower corner, there is a tiny hole. Blow hard into it whilst gently pressing the opposite corner towards you. It will (should!) inflate into a beer bomb.

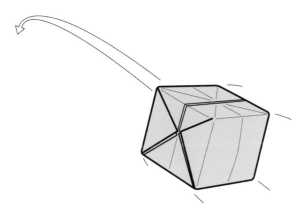

15. Fill through the little hole, allow paper to saturate.
Ready for launching!

Coaster Transformer

Trivial things, coasters, yet they are a vital part of our drinking heritage. Who could imagine sitting at a table without coasters on which to place your beer? There is endless fascination in ensuring your glass is *exactly* in the center of the coaster.

You might think the purpose of a coaster is to soak up spilt beer, thus keeping your best suit dry, but it wasn't always the case. In the good old days, the drinking elite had tankards, with hinged lids designed to keep the flies, spiders and such out of your beer. Poor folk had "ordinary" glasses, so they used a coaster made from felt to cover their ale. In 1880, Robert Sputh of Dresden produced the first cardboard coaster, with a diameter of just over four inches—the size still used today.

Collectors love coasters because they are small, light, colorful, and there are many thousands of different designs and themes. Unlike beer, which you take then return an hour later, coasters are tangible proof that you went into a bar. They make perfect vacation souvenirs and, with very little care, will last forever. Small wonder then that there are so many collectors out there, eager to

track down a 1987 Double Diamond or a 1936 Freising DunklesWeissBier.

Coasters also form a central part in bar games. Given enough, you can construct extensive and impressive walls by laying them against each other (at about 30° for optimum tensile strength). There is also the game of "coaster flicking"—where you balance three mats on the edge of the table, then flick them in the air with the tops of your fingers, catching them as they rotate 180°.

Coasters also function as frisbees, although their flight patterns are fairly erratic and occasionally cause pain and/or damage. This origami design by American Robert Neale is not only a highly decorative coaster, but also magically transforms into a beautiful frisbee. You need eight squares to begin with, but the folding is so simple, you'll complete it almost as quickly as the other designs in this book. Plus, and it's a big plus, your friends will be seriously impressed when you demonstrate it, which is always a good thing.

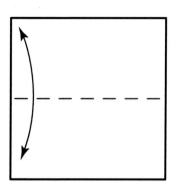

1. Start with a square, white side up, fold in half from side to opposite side, crease and unfold.

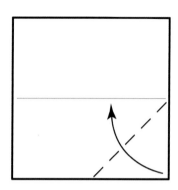

2. Fold the lower-right corner to lie along the crease.

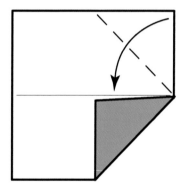

3. Repeat with the upper-right corner.

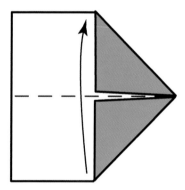

4. Fold in half from top to bottom.

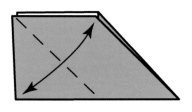

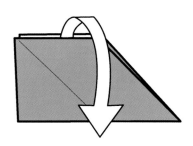

5. Fold the lower-left corner to the upper-right, crease firmly and unfold.

6. Unfold the upper layer.

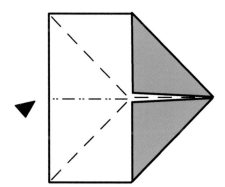

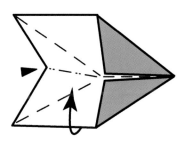

7. Re-fold the paper using the creases exactly as shown.

8. The fold in progress...

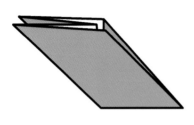

9. And completed. Make seven more, ideally of alternating colors.

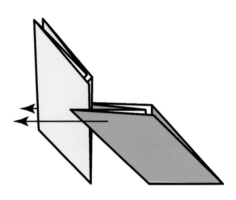

10. Match the positions shown exactly, then slide one around another.

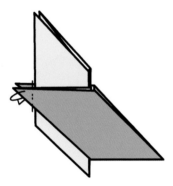

11. Wrap the upper flap behind the first layer.

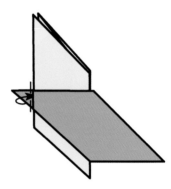

12. Repeat with the matching layer underneath.

13. Continue around with the other six pieces.
If you gently ease the layers outwards, it will expand into a ring.
If you ease them together, a wonderful star beermat is formed.

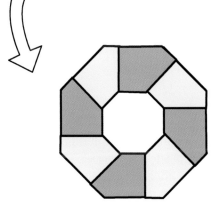 

Barf Bag

As any drinker knows, there are serious implications when drinking to excess (not the least of which is who will pay for it all). Firstly there is the way in which the room beings to spin around before your eyes, technically known as "the spins". Then there is the prospect of your drink returning from whence it came, along with whatever you had for lunch. Yes, we're talking barfing.

In Thailand, barfing is used to help cure drug addiction. At the Tham Krabok monastery, addicts receive a secret potion that makes them ill. They puke together in a row at 7 o'clock sharp, morning and evening for five days, with fellow inmates cheering encouragement for every resulting heave. The success rate is apparently impressive!

In the interest of science, I asked a doctor to explain what happens when we're sick. It begins with a deep breath, the glottis is closed and the larynx raised to open the upper esophageal sphincter. The soft palate is elevated to close off the posterior nares. The diaphragm contracts sharply downwards to create negative pressure in the thorax. This opens the esophagus and the distal esophageal sphincter. At the same time, the diaphragm moves down, the muscles of the abdominal walls contract, squeezing the stomach and causing intragastric pressure. With the pylorus closed and the esophagus open, there's only one place for it to go.

There are numerous euphemisms for this performance, including throwing up, praying to the porcelain god, technicolor yawn, chucking up, puking, spewing, tossing your cooking, ralphing on the big white telephone, make a crustless pizza, barfing, blowing chunks, chundering, hurling, number three, painting the sidewalk, re-visiting dinner and parking the tiger.

Call it what you will, it happens, and it happens in public. What the sophisticated and urbane origami drunk will do is to prepare a receptacle just in case. This can be kept neatly folded in your pocket, then whipped out when the need, or your stomach, arises. Imagine how impressed the ladies will be when you deposit your number three neatly into a newspaper barf bag, then carefully hide it under the table before offering a bag of chips around the table?

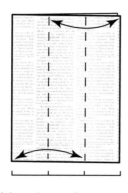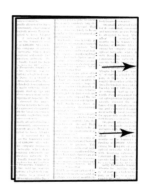

1. Start with a sheet of newspaper, folded in half where it usually is. Fold into thirds, or something like thirds.

2. Turn the paper over and pleat the upper layer on a one-sixth crease.

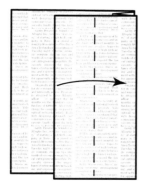

3. Fold a third over.

4. This is the result, turn the paper over.

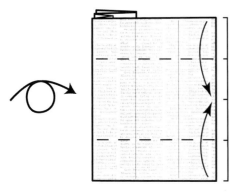 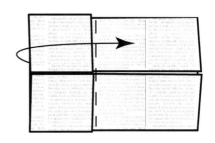

5. Fold upper and lower edges to meet in the center.

6. Fold the thicker, left-hand section to the right.

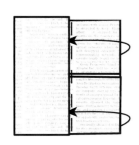 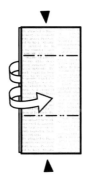 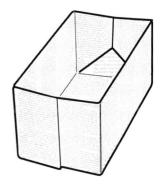

7. Fold the right-hand section over, tucking it deep into the pocket.

8. Open the bag, carefully flattening the sides into position.

9. Ready for—um—use.

Bibliography & Credits

Very Naughty Origami, Nick Robinson
(Universe Publishing, 2004)
The London Pub,
Peter Haydon & Chris Coe
(New Holland Publishers, 2003)
**Man Walks into a Pub:
A Sociable History of Beer**,
Pete Brown (Macmillan, 2003)

This book is dedicated to Mark Burkinshaw, a fellow teenage drinker with unfeasibly long hair (in those days!). It also goes out to all those paper-folders out there who enjoy combining folding with drinking. Not to excess, but simply to loosen the finger joints. All the usual suspects were involved: my family ALL, Daisy, Nick junior, Gomes & Matilda Robinson, several stick insects, my origami family (too numerous to list fully) but includes Lord Brill of Worth Hall, Mick Guy, Saltz und Pfeffer, Mark "no relation" Robinson (proof-reader & test pilot extraordinaire), all@Hurst House, Gareth, Ruth & Rosemary from New Holland Publishers, the Dilshad and Shaans Indian Eateries, Joe, Mick & Wazzer Pointy. David Mead and the Cherry Red squad.

Generous contributors Robert Neale (beermat), Kuni Kasahara (bird), Alex Bateman (full/empty pint), Max Hulme (drunkenness test). The idea for the "Titanic Pint" came from David Mitchell. Belated thanks to Marc Kirschenbaum for "coupling" in *Very Naughty Origami*! The peanut dish, glasses, barf bag, nose, catapult, nodding dog and potato chips were designed by the author, the others are traditional. All contributors retain the copyright in these designs, whether drunk or sober.

For more folding inspiration, try visiting either www.britishorigami.org.uk or www.origami-usa.org and join one, if not both of these worthy societies! A search for origami on the Internet will quickly expose you to unlimited folding pleasure. Purchase of the companion volume *Very Naughty Origami* will give you even more!

The publishers would like to thank the owners of the King of Diamonds (1 Greville Street, London EC1N 8PQ) for opening up early to allow us to photograph the origami in its natural environment—wherever there is alcohol!

First published in the United States of America
in 2005 by UNIVERSE PUBLISHING
A division of Rizzoli International Publications, Inc.
300 Park Avenue South
New York, NY 10010
www.rizzoliusa.com

Originally published in the UK as *Pub Origami*
in 2005 by New Holland Publishers (UK) Ltd
Garfield House
86–88 Edgware Road
London W2 2EA
United Kingdom
www.newhollandpublishers.com

10 9 8 7 6 5 4 3 2 1

ISBN 0-7893-1341-3
Library of Congress Catalog Control Number
2005922589

Editors: Gareth Jones and Ruth Hamilton
Editorial Direction: Rosemary Wilkinson
Photography: Ed Allwright
Artwork: Nick Robinson
Design: Paul Wright
Production: Hazel Kirkman

Reproduction by Modern Age Repro,
Hong Kong
Printed and bound by Craft Print International,
Singapore